J
629
Jon
Jones
Things that go

769653
10.95

| DATE DUE | | | |
|---|---|---|---|
| JE 1 6 '95 | | | |
| | | | |
| | | | |
| | | | |
| | | | |
| | | | |
| | | | |
| | | | |
| | | | |
| | | | |
| | | | |

Ca E

# ittle Book of Questions & Answers

# Things That Go

Manufactured in U.S.A.

8 7 6 5 4 3 2 1

ISBN: 1-56173-471-3

Contributing Writer: Teri Crawford Jones

Cover Illustration: T. F. Marsh

Book Illustrations: Joe Veno

HTS BOOKS
AN IMPRINT OF FOREST HOUSE™
School & Library Edition

769653

## Can an airplane fly to the moon?

An airplane can fly only a few miles above the earth. The moon is much farther away. The moon is in space where there is no air. A plane's engines need air to fly.

## How do people breathe inside an airplane?

High in the sky the air is too cold to breathe. Passengers breathe air that has been heated. Pipes carry the warm air throughout the plane's cabin.

## How does a suitcase get on the right plane?

At the check-in counter, your suitcase gets a tag. The tag tells the baggage handlers where you are going. They put your suitcase on a cart that goes to the right plane.

### Where do fire trucks get water to fight fires?

A pumper truck hooks up to a hydrant that's near the fire. The hydrant's water comes from underground pipes. The truck pumps water from the hydrant into long hoses that the fire fighters hold.

### Why is *ambulance* written backward on the front of an ambulance?

Things look backward in a mirror. The word *ambulance* is written backward so it can be read the right way in a driver's rearview mirror.

### Why do police cars have flashing lights?

The flashing lights on a police car catch our attention even when we do not hear the police car's siren. The flashing lights tell drivers to pull over and stop.

### How do people stay on skateboards?

Skateboarders use their whole body—especially their arms—to keep balanced. Shoes with rubber soles also help to keep skateboarders from slipping off their boards.

### How do the hand brakes on a bicycle work?

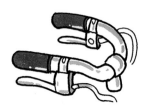

Squeezing the hand brakes makes a pair of small rubber pads grab the rim of each wheel. The rubber pads rub the wheel rims and make the wheels turn slower or stop altogether.

### Why do tricycles have three wheels?

Having three wheels keeps a tricycle balanced—even when nobody is riding it. A tricycle is good pedaling practice for kids who want to ride a bicycle someday!

### Why do you sit backward to row a rowboat?

It is easier to sit backward in a boat so you can pull the oars rather than push them through the water. Watch where you're going!

### Why do canoes tip over so easily?

Canoes are narrow and have rounded bottoms so they move through water easily. This makes them tip over easily, too. When you are in a canoe, you must sit in the middle to stay balanced.

### What do sailboats do if there is no wind?

Many sailboats have small motors to drive them when the wind has died. Without the motor, the boat's sailors would have to wait for the wind to blow again or they would have to row with oars.

## Why do people travel in taxis?

A taxi is a way to get around town if you don't drive or don't have your car with you on a trip. Also, if you are in a crowded city, it is nice not to have to search for a parking spot!

## How is a school bus different from a city bus?

Besides looking different inside and outside, city buses have different schedules than school buses. City buses often run all day and night. School buses usually only run when they are taking students to and from school.

## Why do we pay money to ride a city bus?

The money we pay helps to keep the city buses running. It also helps pay the driver for doing his or her job.

### Why are subways under the ground?

By having the subway train run underground, there is more room on top of the ground. That's important in a crowded city. Also, the noise of the underground train stays underground—and that's nice, too.

### Where is a cable car's cable?

A cable, which is like a metal rope, is hooked to the cable car. The cable is close to the track. A motor pulls the cable and the cable pulls the car along the track.

### What is a freight train?

"Freight" can be anything that needs to be carried from one place to another. Freight trains are loaded with things like machine parts, food, or lumber. Living things are not usually called freight.

## Is a backhoe the same as a bulldozer?

No. A backhoe scoops up dirt and rocks and carries them to another spot. A bulldozer has a big blade on its front that pushes dirt and rocks around and makes the ground smooth.

## Why are bulldozers so big?

Bulldozers do big jobs—they need to be big! They push heavy rocks and move big piles of dirt from place to place. They need lots of weight behind them for that extra-strong push!

## What do cranes do?

A crane is like a very long, very strong arm. It picks up dirt, rocks, and other things and moves them from place to place. Some cranes have strong magnets for picking up scrap metal.

## Why are rockets so loud when they take off?

It takes a lot of power to shoot a rocket into space. Rockets have big engines that blast them into the sky. The engines and the burning fuel make lots of noise!

## What do satellites do?

Some send weather pictures to weather stations on earth. Some send phone calls or television programs around the world. Some satellites are top secret—only a few people know what they do!

## What is a space station?

Some day, space stations will be cities in space. But for now, space stations are like Skylab, where astronauts go for awhile to do experiments in space.

### How do elevator doors know when to open?

When you push the button for the floor you want, you are sending an electrical "message" to the elevator's motor. When the elevator reaches your floor, the doors get the message to open.

### Why do some airports have moving sidewalks?

It can be a long, difficult walk through an airport—especially if you are carrying lots of suitcases. A moving sidewalk will carry you and your suitcases so you will have enough energy to enjoy your trip!

### Where do the escalator steps go?

Escalator steps are connected in a big loop. They flatten out before they go under the floor. They circle around and come up again from the other end.

### Why does a balsa-wood airplane fly?

A balsa-wood plane is very light. It flies because it has wings and a tail like a real airplane. It can do all kinds of loops and tricks in the air!

### Why does a windup toy run down?

Windup toys have a spring inside. By turning the key on the outside of the toy, we wind up that spring. When we let go of the key, the spring unwinds. As the spring unwinds, the toy runs slower until it stops.

### What makes a model train go?

Electricity runs through the train tracks and into the engine's motor. The motor turns the wheels on the engine and the engine pulls the other cars around the track. Toot! Toot!

## Why is a tugboat called a tugboat?

When a big ship is ready to come into a harbor, it stops its own motors and lets a tugboat pull—or "tug"—it in. Ships' motors are too strong to be used in a harbor.

## Why do people use submarines?

Sometimes we use submarines to fight in wars. Subs can hide from enemies by diving deep in the ocean. Sometimes subs are used by scientists who are studying the deep, dark ocean.

## What is below the deck of a big ship?

On a cruise ship, most of the passengers' rooms are below deck. On a battleship, the sailors' quarters are there. Storage areas, pipes, wiring, and airways are under the deck, too.

### Why don't dune buggies get stuck in the sand?

A dune buggy's tires are very wide. The wide wheels help it stay on top of the sand instead of sinking down into it.

### What happens to a convertible car if it rains?

When it begins to rain, the driver of a convertible must stop the car and put up the top. If it rains and no one is around to put up the top, the inside of the car gets very wet!

### How do surfboards go?

First, surfers watch for a good wave. Then they paddle so their boards are in front of where the wave curls over. As the wave rolls toward shore, it pushes the surfers in front of it.

## How does the roller coaster stay on the track?

Many roller coasters have wheels on all four sides of the track. These wheels help hold the cars onto the track at all times. They won't fall even when they are upside down!

## How do merry-go-round horses gallop?

The pole to which each horse is attached is fastened to a crank under the roof of the merry-go-round. A motor makes the ride go around. It also makes the pole go up and down as if the horses are galloping!

## Why don't Ferris-wheel seats turn upside down?

The seats are fastened to the wheel so that they can swing back and forth. When the wheel goes around, the seats hang down because of gravity.

## Why does a train whistle?

Trains whistle to say, "I'm coming down the track! Get off the train track!" The whistle warns people—and perhaps animals—to stay clear and be careful. Train conductors are supposed to sound the whistle every time the train crosses a roadway.